Be An Author

Be An Author

A Guide to the Basics and the Bewares of Getting Published

Diane S. Nine

RAND-SMITH PUBLISHING

BE AN AUTHOR: A Guide to the Basics and the Bewares of Getting Published

By: Diane S. Nine

Print ISBN: 978-1-950544-06-6

Digital ISBN: 978-1-950544-07-3

Registered with the Library of Congress

All attempts have been made to provide accurate information by the author. The information is not intended to give legal advice.

Diane S. Nine, President

Nine Speakers, Inc.

A Full-Service Entertainment Industry

www.ninespeakers.com

Rand-Smith Publishing

www.Rand-Smith.com

Ashland, Va

Printed in the USA

Contents

Dedication

For my friend, Dave Smitherman, writer extraordinaire.

Acknowledgments

A special thanks to my parents, Paul and Susan Nine, for providing me with the best education possible to be able to develop sound writing skills — and for their lifelong support of any and all ventures.

And heartfelt thanks to Rand-Smith Publishing for giving me this opportunity to share my insights about an industry that we all love.

Finally, thanks to all my terrific clients for keeping me employed for more than a couple decades, and for letting me work in an industry I adore.

Introduction

The literary world can be confusing. You want to get a book published, but where do you begin? How do you decide what to write? How do you know if what you write can actually be published? How do you find an agent, and how do you know what to submit to an agent? What is it like to be a published author? How do you publicize and market your book once it is published? I am going to attempt to answer these and other questions in the pages that follow.

There is a great deal of misinformation about getting a book published, what it is like to work with an agent or publisher, and what the process is really like. Clichés and oft repeated "truisms" are handed down from one person to another without any real basis in fact. It is the way people say it is, because this is the conventional wisdom.

Television shows and movies portray agents or publishers giving expensive cars to their authors as a bonus for writing the great American novel. Every writer not only receives an advance for their book, but also receives such a large advance that they can quit their day job and write full time. John Grisham, Tom Clancy, J.K. Rowling, and even William Shakespeare have nothing on the potential success of every would-be author's sales' figures. After all, YOU have all the advice you need from the shows you've watched, the books you've read, and the advice you've been given by your friends — who have seen the same shows and read the same books or articles.

Even authors often embellish about the realities of their own book projects. I can't tell you the number of times

I have overheard a client bragging about how little time it took to get a book published — from the writing, all the way through publication. Trust me when I tell you that the process is SLOW. Well-done writing is, by its very nature, extremely time-consuming. And publishers are notoriously slow given all the tasks that must be completed before the manuscript can even be sent to the printer or the distributor or converted to the various e-book platforms.

In my work, I have also marveled at the myriad of occasions when I have read in the paper or heard on the radio or TV about the generous advance an author received — despite the reality of a small, or nonexistent, advance. My favorite story in this area involves a client who got a six-figure advance (a substantial advance by most standards). By the time the book was released, the author had convinced the media that her publisher gave her a seven-figure advance since her publisher "knew" her book would "outpace" all their other titles for the year. In case you're wondering, the book did well, but based on the number of copies sold, I am sure the publisher is glad they "only" forked over the six-figure advance.

However, not all authors prevaricate. In fact, most authors find themselves in the unfortunate position of relying upon the publishing industry's conventional wisdom — only to be faced with the harsh realities of how the industry REALLY works. I know of more than one author who was blown away by the lack of support given to them by the publisher when the book was finally published. Writers hear about the large publicity machines at the publishing houses. Authors fill out long questionnaires to assist the marketing and publicity departments, listing contacts in the media, membership organizations which might host a book signing, and any other contact who might help sell even one book. After all of this, authors are often disappointed in the utter lack of interest by the publisher in doing anything to push their book. As a result, authors usually end up facing the harsh reality that they are usually on their own, or they will have to work hard to sell books. Every author needs to understand that publishers, by tradition, do not focus their efforts on promoting books in the retail market — though they have plenty of other responsibilities which are integral to a successful book.

Because authors do need to publicize their own books, it can be advantageous to work with a professional publicist. Once again, authors often have unrealistic expectations of what a publicist can do. Authors love to say, “I know Oprah will be interested.” Or, “I want to be on the *Today* show.” In the early days of my career, I would suggest begging the *Today* show, or whatever program du jour. I wanted to please the author and their publisher. I soon met the reality. The authors were unrealistic, AND my friends and media contacts were only interested if they thought the author or book would further a story. I guess I would be the same way if I worked in the media.

Nonetheless, there have been times when I pitched an author and their book and I had to scratch my head. In one instance, a media outlet strung me along, eventually telling me that their company was no longer doing “book” segments. The very next day, I tuned into the show to see what type of programming would be of interest to them. There it was on the first part of their show: a book segment. Go figure.

Needless to say, most agents aren’t actually equipped to work as publicists, so authors undoubtedly find more success with professional publicists who work full-time in this area.

However, despite it all, most agents have a love for books, and the publishing industry. As the American comedian and actor, Groucho Marx, once said, "Outside of a dog, a man's best friend is a book. Inside of a dog, it's too dark to read."

So — I would like to share my love of the literary world with you. I will give you my insights about the realities of getting a book published, and I hope my "basics and bewares" will inspire your bestseller. At the very least, you will have a better understanding of how to work with an agent, what to expect as an author, and possibly, how to get your book headed to a publishing house.

Happy writing!

1.

The Agent – Background

Agents, as in most professions, come from all walks of life, and a variety of backgrounds. I grew up in Michigan in a family of entrepreneurs. My parents met on the debate team while they were in college (you can only imagine what the "discussions" were like in our household with two parents and one child who come by debating naturally). My parents eloped on a debate trip while they were still in college. My dad went to law school at night while working a day job at Chrysler. By the time I was old enough to go to school, my dad started his own law firm, and because my parents grew up poor, there was barely enough money to pay another attorney's salary — let alone pay any support staff. As a result, my mom and grandmother went to work at "the office" performing all the duties other than practicing law.

I had my own room at the office where I went after school. I had the run of the place, and my play dates often joined me at the office. We used to think it was really cool to get a snack or meal at the restaurant in the office building where I was allowed to sign my name to the bill since my dad had an account. I learned a lot about hard work and sacrifice in those early days of my life. As an only child growing up in an adult setting, I also learned to entertain myself. Thus, I began my constant reading habit, and my love of anything on the written page. By the time I was in fourth grade, I was "writing" my own books, complete with poorly drawn illustrations (I am still unable to even draw an adequate stick figure). I would use file folders with holes punched on the left side as the book jacket, and yarn or string tied through the holes to hold the book together. I'm sure my dad's employees (he was ultimately able to hire some as his firm grew) particularly enjoyed my presence when I asked them to buy copies of my books for 25 cents.

Meantime, my parents had their eyes on other businesses, in addition to the law firm. We began making a four-hour drive from the Detroit suburbs to northern Michigan almost every weekend so that my dad could do the legal work for the first ABC affiliate television station "up north" — as Michiganders say. These long, boring car rides presented even more opportunities for my ever-increasing reading habit, and by the time the TV station was up and running, I spent time sitting in the studio, observing the goings on. This changed the nature of my own "books" — with many of the plots based upon action in the local TV world.

Even after my dad helped found the station, we continued our treks "up north" when my parents decided to develop a large plot of land into the largest resort in the mid-west. My reading habit was bigger than ever since it was more boring than ever to sit in meetings about some resort that would exist in the future (though ultimately the resort had its benefits once it was built — and all my friends were able to enjoy all the "free" activities and amenities since I was the owner's child). Despite all the fun available, my friends and I still found time for reading, and sometimes we "co-authored" books together. At least I don't have any recollection of trying to sell our "books" to the resort employees as I had done with the law firm staff.

Nobody can grow up in this type of environment without

placing a high value on education. In grade school, as my parents became slightly more affluent, they put me in Cranbrook Schools, a private prep school with high academic standards. As a result, there was never any question as to whether I would attend college. In addition, with a lawyer-father who accomplished so much at a young age, I was certain that law school was the path for me.

However, law school was to be delayed by a year after college. My parents had always been active in politics on the periphery, and I too caught the political bug. As a high school teenager, I secured an internship in Jimmy Carter's White House doing research and writing. It was a heady experience, and I had found a way to combine my love of reading and writing with my enthusiasm for all things political. After several summers in the White House, President Carter lost the election. I then used every summer and January Term from high school and college to do additional internships in Washington, DC, working such places as former Senator Don Riegle's office, Senator Levin's office, and the Washington bureau of CNN in its infancy — to name a few. I had been bitten by Potomac fever, and I had made a lot of valuable contacts while honing my writing skills.

I moved to DC permanently right out of college to go to law school. However, a more enticing opportunity would present itself, causing me to postpone my advanced degree for a year. The 1984 presidential season was in full swing. I had volunteered some time with the Mondale campaign the previous summer during my full-time internship with CNN (TV hours are not necessarily nine to five, leaving some time to fill during regular work hours as a young, energetic woman). Upon settling into my new life in Washington, I decided to volunteer again for the campaign, which was now heading toward the Democratic

Convention, and the subsequent general election. I was stunned that I was offered a staff position as a press secretary at the age of 22, and it was a chance to be in the thick of politics that I couldn't refuse. George Washington University's Law School agreed to defer me for a year to take advantage of my campaign opportunity, and I was in heaven.

I had a blast on the campaign and was beginning to reconsider my decision to go to law school at all — much to the dismay of my family and some friends. I was really learning the ins and outs of the political life, and I loved it. Somewhere along the way (maybe when it started to become apparent that my candidate had zero probability of winning), I realized that politics could be rewarding, but it could also mean that I might be constantly looking for a new job. An unending life of continual job hunting ultimately sounded worse than going back to school.

Law school began the fall after the campaign came to an abrupt end with the votes going to Ronald Reagan in a landslide. Torts, contracts, criminal law, and constitutional law, among other classes seemed like torture, even though the course work came relatively easily to me. I longed for political conversations with my colleagues and friends in the media. I didn't know how I would be able to put up with three years of more legal ethics, trusts and estates, media law, labor law, and the rest of it.

I began to find new meaning in the well-known Shakespeare saying, "The first thing we do, let's kill all the lawyers." That is, until some people from my political world started asking me for help with some small legal issues. Almost all of these "issues" fell under the broad umbrella of entertainment law, including some which related to the literary world. I was back in my element! With a professor's supervision, I was doing quasi-legal work in an area in which I excelled and enjoyed. I knew I could earn that J.D. after all.

By my third and final year of law school, my classmates were all dressed up in suits, interviewing for jobs with every law firm imaginable. The school career advisor was extremely frustrated with me, and friends and family were concerned that I had no desire to go on these interviews. But I grew up (literally) in my father's law firm, and I knew this wasn't for me. Billable hours, clients with nothing but problems, billable hours, unending research as a new associate, and more billable hours. Who in their right mind would want to be responsible for every 15 minutes of their time, or be accountable for a possible court loss when people's well-being might be at stake?

Suddenly a light bulb went off. Why not start my own agency, and continue with the "clients" I had been assisting as a student? My own business would be a way to stay in the loop with my political friends (and foes!), utilize my law degree, and work with writers.

In 1988, freshly minted from law school, I opened Nine Speakers, Inc. with the handful of clients I had already been advising. "Agenting" tends to be a substantially word of mouth business, so the company quickly expanded, and we now represent people across the world in the literary, lecture, film, television, and theatrical arenas. The majority of our work is in the literary area, and despite the (sometimes) difficult nature of this timeless, yet rapidly changing industry, I (almost) always look forward to getting to my desk each morning.

Thomas Jefferson was truly a wise man when he told John Adams in 1815: "I cannot live without books."

2.

Finding an Agent & the Agency Agreement

The American actor, singer, and comedian, Groucho Marx, once remarked, "I wish to be cremated. One tenth of my ashes shall be given to my agent, as written in our contract."

The sentiment expressed by Marx is a common feeling among most people. Agents are thought of as bottom feeders, living happily in their own cesspools. They care about no one but themselves, and their only goal in life is to cut a deal to make millions of dollars. Deals are made to further an agent's bottom line, even if the deal isn't beneficial to the client being represented. These shark-like, unethical crooks will do anything to capitalize on their clients' desires to become famous and make it big. The only thing worse than an agent is an attorney, and the only thing worse than an attorney is an agent with a law degree (I have the double whammy as an agent-lawyer!). Right? Well, maybe.

It is true that there's a myriad of "bad agent" stories. I hear them with some frequency from potential clients who have felt "burned" by a previous relationship with an agent. Sometimes these tales ring true, but other times, it seems that the complaining author hasn't held up their end of the bargain. Some examples of the bad agent and the bad author follow.

The Bad Agent: I have a client who obtained a book deal with an imprint of HarperCollins through the efforts of another agent. The deal seemed great on the face of it. There was a decent-sized advance (with the payment divided into thirds, as is often the case). The royalties were on the generous end as far as publishing goes, and the author had an adequate amount of time to complete the manuscript (without having to wait years for the book to see the light of day). All seemed well — until the author began to wonder when she would receive the first third of the advance which was contractually due within a certain period of time after signing the publisher's contract. As is standard operating procedure, all of the monies due from the publisher to the author were to be paid to the agent. The agent was supposed to take his fifteen percent off the top and disburse the rest of the payment to the author. The author began leaving messages for her agent, to no avail. After considerable time, and subsequent to the timeframe when the second third of the advance was due, the author asked the agent about her money when she finally reached him by phone. The agent had no explanation other than to say that he had spent the advance! Clearly, the agent in this scenario was a crook, and deserved the snake-like reputation that so many people feel toward agents.

The Bad Author: In two instances in the last year or so, I have had unreasonable situations with authors. In both cases, I sold the books for the authors being represented. As you probably know, there is no money exchanged up front between an agent and an author. Therefore, agents must rely on 15 to 20 percent (I am still working off of 15 percent) of any advances and royalties to make a living. In these scenarios, both authors sent me emails asking me to resign as their agents as soon as the books began earning royalties. When I asked the authors if they were unhappy with me for some reason, I got answers such as, "I like you, and you did a great job selling my book. However, I thought it would be better to just be friends." Obviously, these authors were trying to cut me out of money which I was owed, and money which was the only way in which I would be paid for my work successfully performed. While I was ultimately compensated for my efforts (the authors' attorneys told them they didn't have a legal leg to stand on), I certainly didn't appreciate the authors' unethical behavior. All people should be paid fairly for work properly completed.

So, as you can see, there can be issues on both sides of the equation. I could fill a whole book with stories akin to the ones above, but I think you get the idea. The bigger issue here is: How can authors (and agents) be sure of a good working relationship, and prevent scenarios like those above? Like most things in life, there are no guarantees. But there are some steps that can be taken to mitigate the possibility of an unfortunate problem down the road.

Researching the Agent

First, both the agent and author should feel comfortable with one another. If an agent is interested in representing a writer, both parties should have a lengthy telephone conversation. You can glean a lot of information just by getting to know each other, and by asking questions. If you live in the same geographic area, you can also see if the agent will meet with you in person, but most initial contacts are done by phone.

For instance, I recently had a discussion with a potential client whose book proposal appeared well-written, clever, original, and highly marketable. During our phone call, I asked the writer how he envisioned promoting his book if the project moved forward. In a harsh tone, the author said, "I have no intention of doing anything, other than to complete the manuscript. The rest of it is your problem. I am busy." Unfortunately, no books have potential in the marketplace without some effort on the part of the writer. When I was unable to reason with the author in question, I declined to represent him. He simply was not a good fit with the way in which I work.

From an author's reference point, there is even more to be learned from the potential agent. The author should ask whether the agent likes their work, and why. Obviously, if the person representing you isn't excited about your book, the agent will not have the requisite enthusiasm to sell the book, to assist in promoting the book, to help find book stores to sell the book for signings, and to continue to advocate on your behalf with the publisher (and there are ALWAYS issues which require advocacy!).

The author should also ask questions about the publishing industry — and the agent should be able to answer most of those questions. Of course, all people, no matter what field they work in, are sometimes stumped by a question on a topic they have never dealt with before. But the agent should be able to adequately reply to the vast majority of inquiries.

In addition, the agent should be able to run through the publishing process, the agency agreement, and the publishing contract. They should be knowledgeable about the financial side of the publishing business — including how the agent gets paid (it is, with some exceptions, unethical for an agent to accept any money from the author upfront). The agent should be well versed in how advances and royalties work and should be capable of going into some detail.

The author should also ask the agent if they have some publishers in mind who might be interested in your manuscript, and if the agent has a specific format by which the work is submitted to the publishers. Further, you should find out how the agent will keep you informed throughout the process. For instance, in my company, we email our clients every time we get feedback from a publisher about a client's book proposal by simply forwarding what we receive from the publishing house (or if the publisher calls, we take notes, and quote the publisher in the email to the author).

Obviously, it is in the interest of the author to find out how long the agent has been in business, how they became an agent (and why), what genres the agent has worked in previously, and if the agent is willing to provide examples of books that have been successfully published that were represented by their agency. This is no different than the kinds of information exchanged during any job interview or colleague collaboration in the workplace.

Finally, in your discussion with your potential agent, the agent should acknowledge some of the pitfalls, trials, and tribulations in the publishing industry. The only way for an author to make educated decisions is to be informed, and the author should be aware of some of the possible problems down the road if they write a book (and succeed in getting it published). Like most areas of work, the literary world is not trouble free. If an agent acts like the book industry is one, happy panacea, they are not truthful — and you should run in the opposite direction. This is not to say, however, that writers, agents, and publishers aren't happy in their work. You should just be aware of all angles of the industry in case problems arise.

The second area writers can use in evaluating possible agents is the Internet. You can, of course, google the agent and the agency. You can also look at the agency's web site. In addition, there are a lot of web sites that offer general information about publishing, and many of them list information on agents (more on these sites below). Believe it or not, there are still books available for purchase that list agents, too.

However, in your search for an agent, I would advise a word of caution when using the Internet as a resource. While most web sites are generally reliable, some of them have inaccurate information, and quite a few of them list information without ever even talking with the agents they discuss. In fact, there is one web site that has a thread complaining about me. I do not know any of the people writing about me (with the exception of a publisher whom I have worked with — who attempts to set the record straight), nor have I ever spoken with or met any of the allegedly unhappy writers. I am certainly not perfect, but it bothers me that some great authors might not consider my representation based on false information. Because everything on the Internet stays there forever, and the usual rules and laws of defamation don't seem to regularly apply, it is important to look up agents in more than one place. It can also be beneficial to contact an agent and ask them about the derogatory material on a web site.

With that said, there are some web sites that seem reliable (in my humble opinion) in searching for an agent. The sites I prefer are those that give straight forward information in an organized manner. They don't allow off-color complaining, and they ask the agent's permission to be listed. There are quite a few sites available, and I'm sure I don't know all of them.

Therefore, I will leave you with two suggestions. My favorite literary website is Publishers Marketplace (www.publishersmarketplace.com), and one of the better known sites is the Literary Marketplace, known in the industry as the LMP (www.literarymarketplace.com).

In addition to all of the above, don't forget that friends, family, and colleagues can be great resources for locating an agent if any of them have ever written a book (and are pleased with their agent-author relationship).

Understanding the Agency Agreement

Once you have located an agent to represent you, the agent should ask you to sign an agency agreement. You should never work with an agent who doesn't present a contract. After all, there's money involved in legitimate book deals, and even friends and family often fight over money. It is beneficial to you and the agent to have all the terms in a signed agreement.

Most agency contracts are similar in nature, and many of the clauses overlap with those you will find in publishing agreements. The primary warranties from the author say that the author's work is original, and they didn't rip off anyone else's work. The agent usually warranties that she or he will use their best efforts to secure the best deal for the author.

The contract should also address how the agent will be compensated, and this is typically 15 to 20 percent of whatever happens with the book. If the agent isn't able to sell the book, no money should have been exchanged upfront, so nobody should be out anything — except for valuable time.

Usually, the agent's percentage is construed broadly, and includes anything that "flows" from the book. For example, the following would typically be included if they are related to the book: any form the book can take (e.g., e-books, audio books, hardcover books, paperback books, Internet books, etc.), television shows or series, films, theatrical shows, etc. There are so many ways to turn books into ancillary projects, and all of this is a part of the agent's economic benefit, too. The reasoning behind this is that the author most likely wouldn't have had anything if the agent hadn't first sold the book. However, if all of this is included, you should retain an agent who has the know how to try to get the book optioned, etc. Frankly, most books only exist as a book itself, but you can never tell if your book will be the next award-winning play or movie.

The agency agreement should have an "exclusivity" period included in it, so that neither the author, nor the agent, are stuck with one another forever if the relationship doesn't work out as envisioned. These clauses are anywhere from six months to several years. My contract is for one year — which I believe gives the agent a fair amount of time to sell the book but allows the writer to move on to another agent if there aren't any results. Agency agreements can also be renewed if both parties want to give it a little longer to see what happens.

Many agency agreements also have option clauses for an author's next book. This is normal since many authors take time to build an audience, and often times, second or third books sell better. The author would not have the ability to write second books if the agent had not sold their first work.

Authors should be aware that agents are not required to hand over lists of acquiring editors at publishing houses if the contract is terminated, and they certainly are not going to give you contact information for the publishers they contacted on your behalf. Agents make a living, in part, due to the relationships they have developed, and they aren't going to give this information to you on a silver platter. It is proprietary. However, agents should provide the author with the names of publishing companies and imprints who agreed to consider your book proposal.

As mentioned earlier, there are some standard clauses in

agency contracts, but there can also be some differences from agent-to-agent. My contract has evolved over time as various issues arose, and I have a good reason why each clause is included in the agreement. For example, early in my career, I didn't realize that, as a whole, publishers do not want to hear from authors with any frequency — and sometimes not at all. Unbeknownst to me, I had a client who also had a ghostwriter. Apparently, the author and the ghost writer were calling the publisher several times a day. I eventually received a call from the publisher, saying the publisher would pull the deal if she ever heard from my clients again.

Publishers usually like to communicate with the author through their agent. This can also be helpful to the author since the agent is intimately familiar with all of the rules, traditions, and customs as to how things work in the literary world, and this is especially true if your agent is also an attorney. Think about it. If you hire a lawyer, you aren't the one communicating with the opposing counsel or with the person suing or defending a law suit brought by you. Instead, your attorney does all the talking, emailing, and "snail mailing" letters. As a result of the scenario above, I now have a clause in my boilerplate agency agreement that says the author agrees they will not communicate with their publisher without my permission. Besides, authors should WANT their agents involved at all times — the agent is the author's advocate!

In other words, writers shouldn't be worried if there are some "different" clauses in the agency contract. However, the agent (or their counsel) should be able to explain each and every clause if the author doesn't understand something. In fact, no legal document should ever be signed without understanding what is being signed.

Many authors choose to have an attorney review the

agency agreement before placing their "John Hancock" on the document, and agents should have no objection to this. In fact, I think it is a good idea to have your own counsel look over the contract before it is signed.

With this said, many agents are inflexible in agreeing to changes in their contracts, and it is their right. The most important thing to remember is that you should understand what the contract means, and then make an informed decision as to whether you want to sign it. If you or your attorney don't think the agreement should be executed, and the agent won't agree to proposed changes, then it is best to try to find another agent — or decide if you can live with the terms of the agreement.

Finally, authors should know that the law has become rather specialized. Therefore, the attorney who drew up your will, or handled your divorce, may not be well-versed in agency or publishing agreements. You should be certain your attorney understands intellectual property rights, as well as the standards and norms in the publishing industry.

An agent can be a valuable asset and resource, but writers should feel comfortable with their representation — so agents should be chosen carefully.

3.

What an Agent Wants & the Book Proposal

So, what do agents look for in deciding whether or not to represent an author? How can you insure you will be able to land an agent? It might not be as hard as you imagine if you follow some simple guidelines with your writing, and how you present your writing. However, writing (with the intent of getting published) can be a bit like playing the lottery — the more you play, the better your chances of winning. In fact, I have a client who started crying when I told her we finally had an offer from a publishing house. When she composed herself, she responded to the good news by saying, "It feels like I just won the lottery!" Some of this is because of the old cliché, "Beauty is in the eye of the beholder."

Admittedly, evaluating book proposals and manuscripts involves a certain amount of subjectivity. Examples of authors who were repeatedly turned down by agents and publishers abound — many of whom went on to become some of the most successful authors in the history of the modern literary world. John Grisham comes to mind. He spent years trying to interest someone in A TIME TO KILL, to no avail. He was rejected by nearly thirty publishers. Finally, an unknown, independent publisher, Wynwood Press, picked up the book, and did a small print run of 5,000 copies. Grisham began writing his second book the day after he finished his first manuscript. THE FIRM was published by Bantam Dell (part of Random House) in 1991 — and the rest is history. The book spent 47 weeks on *The New York Times'* bestseller list, and it was adapted for a feature film. John Grisham was on the map, and despite his early trouble getting published, he has gone on to write a seemingly endless number of legal thrillers. For a while, I thought the Random House offices in New York even looked like a shrine to Grisham!

Other well-known authors have similar stories, too. For example, Tom Clancy's first military, espionage thriller, THE HUNT FOR RED OCTOBER, was published in 1984 by the Naval Institute Press — not exactly one of the giant New York conglomerate publishing houses. However, these days, Clancy's main character in his first book, Jack Ryan, is essentially a household name.

Bestselling author of the HARRY POTTER series, J.K. Rowling also started slow. She supposedly began working diligently on the first book in the series when she was 26 years old in 1991. The book was finally published in the United Kingdom by Bloomsbury Children's books in 1997 for a whopping amount of approximately $4,000 — hardly an amount worthy of what the books could eventually earn. Of course, Rowling subsequently made it big when Scholastic bought the American rights, and Rowling's first three books in her series simultaneously landed in the top three slots on the *New York Times'* bestseller list.

Interestingly, John Grisham, Tom Clancy, and J.K. Rowling are the only three authors to sell 2 million copies of a book in the first printing in the 1990's. Ultimately, luck was with them after their initial struggles to get published, and certain publishers' subjective tastes worked well for these authors.

Sometimes evaluating the viability of book proposals or

manuscripts reminds me of what the U.S. Supreme Court once said about defining obscenity: "You know it when you see it." However, disregarding the elements of chance and human opinion, there are some hints to help authors secure an enthusiastic agent (and publisher).

Deciding What to Write

First, every possible writer needs to write because they love to write. Nobody should attempt to author a book because the literary industry appears glamorous, or because your best friend or family member was able to get a book published. Nor should you try to write a book because you are in a financial predicament. I can't tell you the number of times I have heard people tell me they want to be published so they can make bucket loads of money. This is not a good reason to write. Sometimes there's a lot of money in publishing. Other times, authors don't fare quite as well, and the financial side is disappointing. In addition, if it is painful to sit down at your keyboard, writing is not for you (though it is perfectly normal to occasionally have "writer's block"). In sum, like most things in life, you will meet with more success if you enjoy what you are doing. As American science fiction and popular science author, Isaac Asimov, remarked, "I write for the same reason I breathe, because if I didn't, I would die." Or, as Britain's Poet Laureate, William Wordsworth, once said, "Fill your paper with the breathings of your heart."

Second, authors should write what they know, and write in a genre they like to read. People are always better at things with which they have some familiarity, and agents and publishers can usually tell if an author is working in an area they don't really understand. This is not to say that you can't enhance your knowledge for the topic you are writing about through research and interviews.

There's always room to learn no matter your topic — and everyone needs to look up certain facts and figures. As a rule, though, Irish-born British novelist, C.S. Lewis, put it best when he said, "Write what you want to read."

Third, writers should be cognizant of how they go about telling their story, and how they move the action ahead. One of the biggest mistakes inexperienced authors make is TELLING the reader about the action in a book. Instead, authors should SHOW the reader the action through the plot, characters, and dialogue. Telling the reader what happens doesn't create interest in the same way as showing the progression in the story, and agents and publishers are unlikely to take on manuscripts that are a recitation of what happens in the book. As Anton Chekhov once said, "Don't tell me the moon is shining; show me the glint of light on broken glass."

Fourth, writers need to think back to their school days, and create an outline before engaging in the actual writing — just like your old English teacher required. Start with a general, broad outline. Gradually, fill in the outline with more and more specific information until you have a real sense of the structure and flow of the book. You should know how the manuscript progresses.

For non-fiction, the author should know the theme and point to the book. There should be some basis to your arguments or facts, and you should know where you will get the information for the ideas you posit in the manuscript. You should be able to back up any declarative statements made in your writing through sources or interviews.

In the case of fiction, the writer's outline should reflect the entire story. You should know the beginning, middle, and end of the book in a general way. Be aware of how the plot will progress and get to know your characters. Give them personalities, and human traits. Feel the characters as though they are real. Think of Mark Twain when he remarked, “The people in the story (characters) shall be alive, except in the case of the corpses, and the reader should be able to tell the corpses from the others.”

Evaluating Submissions

More detailed writing tips and hints will follow in Section II of this book, but I want to leave you with a few final thoughts about other areas agents take into consideration when evaluating book proposals and manuscripts.

First and foremost, agents want to see good material. This includes interesting, original ideas — or at least a new take on previously explored ideas. In today’s world, it’s not terribly difficult to check out the competition to determine if others have already written extensively on the subject you are considering. Authors can google, and search Amazon, Barnes & Noble online, or quite a few other Internet outlets. Even if your book idea has already been done, it doesn’t necessarily mean you can’t work with the idea to develop it into something entirely different. If this is the case, you will need to let potential agents know how and why your manuscript differs from similar books in the marketplace.

It may seem obvious, but in addition to looking for a good idea, agents (and publishers) will evaluate and scrutinize the writing in a book proposal and manuscript. There are two aspects that will be considered. The first, which doesn’t involve any subjectivity, is how well the writing has been copy-edited. Just as you might receive a lower grade in school if you turned in a paper filled with typos, incorrect grammar, or incorrect punctuation agents will frown upon these errors. Generally, it is usually worthwhile to review your work several times for typos before submitting any material to an agent. Many authors choose to hire a professional editor to go over their work and make corrections. Blatant errors reflect a lack of caring, and agents are not inclined to work with lazy or uncaring writers.

The second aspect considered in evaluating writing is clearly more subjective but is equally important. Namely, is the writing great, or is it merely adequate? How "readable" is the manuscript? Does the writing draw in the reader so that he or she wants more? In order to answer these questions, authors can impose on friends and family to honestly give an assessment of the writing — and the key here is to ask your readers for their HONEST comments. In addition, there are also professional editors who can help improve your writing style, as well as numerous writing workshops around the country.

Beyond a good idea and excellent writing, agents look at the author's background. Authors who are enthusiastic and appear excited to promote their book if it is published are preferred. In fact, authors who have creative ideas for promotion, or who have connections in the media or at organizations that will host book signings may have a leg up on others.

Most importantly, agents are interested in authors who really have something to say, and agents (and publishers) are always looking for that one book that can stand out from the pack.

Creating a Proposal

Once you have completed your manuscript, or at least a substantial portion of it, you will need to put together a proposal, along with a query letter, to send to agents. I recommend working on the book proposal first since you can use sections of it for your cover letter.

I am sure that different agents have different submission requirements, and there is no right or wrong way to put together a proposal. Below, I will discuss the book proposal format which has been developed and amended over the last many years in my company. It is the same format we use to submit material to publishers, so at least the author only has to figure out how to organize the material once! Usually submissions are sent as Word attachments via email. Following is the book proposal format I recommend:

COVER PAGE

This page should only include the title, the author(s) (and any illustrators), the copyright symbol, and the year. It need not include any personal or contact information. This should be included in the body of the email you send with the proposal and manuscript as Word attachments. Do not use headers or footers. Do not add graphics, photos, or other images. If you have an idea for cover art, this is something you should discuss when you have an agent. While publishers usually consider authors' ideas for cover art, they ultimately make the decision.

TABLE OF CONTENTS

This section is optional, but it can be helpful to the agent or publisher looking at the proposal in case the reader wants to review sections of the proposal in a different order than that with which the proposal sections are presented. It can also be useful if the reader wants to revisit certain sections or evaluate specific sections with colleagues. So, you can decide if you would like to include a Table of Contents, but if you do, be sure the pages in the proposal actually correspond to the pages listed in your Table of Contents. Obviously, you should number the pages of the proposal.

SHORT SUMMARY or BOOK "BLURB"

This section should be one to two short paragraphs and should read much like the jacket description of a published book. Think marketing! It should be short and catchy, while conveying the main theme(s) of the manuscript. Your succinct description should grab the reader, making them want to read more of the proposal.

GENRE

List three categories your book could be listed under. Do not list such categories as "novel" or "non-fiction." Rather, list specific categories such as "political thriller" or "memoir" or "self-help" or "business." If you are not sure where your work falls, look at similar books online to get a sense of the broad categories.

ANTICIPATED WORD COUNT

Publishers focus on the number of words, not pages. This is because when the font size or dimensions of a bound book are changed, it changes the page count.

HOW LONG TO COMPLETE MANUSCRIPT

How long will it take you to complete the manuscript if it isn't already done? Your answer should be less than 3 months, or it is already completed.

COMPETITIVE TITLES

What books have been published that are similar to your work, and how is your book different? Give at least three examples. Do not say "nothing similar has ever been published."

LONG SUMMARY

This section is extremely important since this is your opportunity to tell the agent (and ultimately the publisher) what your manuscript is about in a more detailed way. However, this section should not be a book within a book, either. It should be a relatively brief description of your work and should be one to two pages in length.

CHAPTER-BY-CHAPTER SUMMARY

Write two to three lines describing each chapter's contents.

AUTHOR BIO

This section should tell the reader who the author is, and should highlight any aspects of your schooling, career, or other writing projects that are relevant to your manuscript. You should point out anything in your background that gives you credibility as an author on the topic upon which you have chosen to write. In addition, if you have a job or something else about you that would be useful in promoting a book, this should be included here (though you will also cover some of this territory in the Marketing section below). If there is a co-author, illustrator, or ghost writer, a short bio should be included, as well. This section should be no longer than two pages.

MARKETING AND PUBLICITY

This section should let the agent know that you will be an avid participant in selling your own book if it is published. Unfortunately, the vast majority of publishers do not take an active role in promoting books once they are in the retail marketplace. Therefore, it is imperative that the writer let the agent and publisher know of any ideas you may have to market and publicize your book. For instance, include any organizations, professions, or people who might be interested in the work. You should discuss the three general areas for marketing and publicity: traditional media, Internet media including social networking, as well as a website dedicated to the book), and in-person book signings. Finally, if you can set aside some money to pay a publicist, you should indicate your willingness to do so. Most agents are able to recommend a publicist who is reasonably priced and familiar with book promotion.

MEDIA HOOKS WHEN BOOK IS PUBLISHED

List at least three media hooks. Be as succinct as possible. For example, what would a publicist tell the *Today* show to convince them to have you on? Are there any holidays for which your book would make a perfect gift? Are there any on-going news stories for which your book would be relevant? Is there anything that would help your book get media attention?

SAMPLE CHAPTERS AND MANUSCRIPT

If your manuscript is finished, and EDITED, this is the section to put your work. If the manuscript is not complete, but you have enough of a start on it to give the reader a "feel" for your writing and storyline, you can include sample chapters (which should be carefully edited). Each chapter must be clearly delineated, especially if the chapters included do not read consecutively. Sometimes it might be necessary to write a short description of the action or detail that takes place before a particular sample chapter. This can be accomplished by putting a descriptive sentence or two in brackets just before the chapter in question. If you are relying on sample chapters, as opposed to the completed manuscript, the author should include at least fifty pages (single spaced, with two spaces between paragraphs). In the case of sample chapters, it is also advisable to continue writing your manuscript since, often times, an agent will ask to see more of the work before agreeing to representation. Generally, the more of the work submitted to an agent, the better. While it seems clear, for what it's worth, the more an agent has to consider, the easier it is to determine the possible viability of the book.

PHOTOS

This section is optional, and its inclusion is dependent upon the type of book and/or author. Only include photos if they are relevant to your book, and only if you have the rights and permissions to the pictures. For instance, if you are writing a book about President Obama, and you have photos of the President with you (or others), and you have the rights, the pictures are most likely a good inclusion in the proposal. If your book is on a topic unrelated to President Obama, there is no point to showing off your presidential pics,.

If you are going to include photos or drawings, the author should be aware that the number of pictures in the proposal must be limited to a small number. This is due to the fact that almost everything in the literary world is delivered via email, and not everyone or every company has a gigantic bandwidth. Therefore, only a limited selection of photos can be sent in one email. And, agents and publishers don't like to receive numerous emails on the same project. We get far too many emails, and it is hard to stay organized if there are many emails from the same author — many of which probably don't show up consecutively in the email inbox.

If you think it is important for the agent to understand that the author has a large selection of photos or illustrations (particularly in the case of children's picture books), the author/illustrator can describe the drawings, paintings, or photos in a separate section, or on the page where the material actually belongs. You also can put a link to the other photos in Dropbox or another online storage site.

HISTORY OF BOOK

Has the manuscript ever been self-published or published by a traditional publisher previously? If so, do you have the rights? Who published it, and when was it published? Detail the number of books sold (note that this can be verified, so it is not a good idea to exaggerate). If the work has been published before, why are you seeking a "new" publisher? Please note that a previously self-published or published book is even more difficult to sell, and this may be a turn-off to agents and publishers.

ANYTHING THAT HELPS SELL THE BOOK

Each author and each manuscript is slightly different, so if you have any ideas for sections not mentioned above, you should feel free to include them if they are relevant to your book.

WORKS WITH ILLUSTRATIONS

The illustrations should be where they actually belong in the manuscript. If you are only including samples of the illustrations, on the pages where you are not providing a sample, you should provide a description [in brackets] of what the illustration will be in the spot where it belongs in the manuscript. Note that usually only one or two illustrations can be emailed due to bandwidth. Be sure to fill out the other sections of the proposal above, too.

CHILDREN'S PICTURE BOOKS

The manuscript should be thirty-two pages (plus a front and back cover). Note that this is an exception where the publisher is more concerned with the standard page count than the word count. Each page should contain the words that belong on that page, along with the accompanying illustrations. On the pages where you don't have sample illustrations, you should provide a description [in brackets] of what the illustration will be in the spot where it belongs in the manuscript. If you have all the illustrations completed, it is possible to create a low-resolution PDF file or send the work through Dropbox, but you should ask the agent if this is acceptable before sending it this way. Be sure to fill out the other sections of the proposal above, too.

FORMAT

The author should submit the book proposal in one continuous document in Microsoft Word. If you have the latest, brand new version of Word, it might be advisable to "dumb down" the file and save the document in the previous version of the software. Everyone knows how frustrating it is to be unable to open or read a document on a computer.

My company prefers to have the proposal single spaced in a twelve point, easily read font. Paragraphs should have two spaces in between them. However, other agents might like to see everything double spaced, so it is best to check on the submission requirements and format before sending off your masterpiece.

COPYRIGHT

If you would like to formally copyright your work (which does give you the best legal protection), you can get the form from the web at www.copyright.gov/forms. Choose Form TX. Don't forget to send a copy of your work, as well as the required fee, with the form you fill out.

QUERY LETTER

After the book proposal is completed, you will need to include a query letter in the body of an email before contacting an agent. Since all your hard work on the proposal has already been done, I suggest using portions of it in your letter.

Begin by saying you are looking for an agent's representation for your work. Give a succinct description of your manuscript (use the short summary from the proposal). Tell the agent a little bit about yourself (use all or part of the author bio from the proposal).

Let the agent know you are excited at the prospect of being published, and you are ready and willing to do whatever it takes to be published — and will promote the book if it is successfully published (use parts of marketing and publicity from the proposal).

Conclude your query letter by thanking the agent for their time and consideration, and by offering to send your book proposal. If you are contacting more than one agent at a time, you also should alert the agents that the query received is a multiple submission.

Query letters should be relatively short (no more than one to two pages), but long enough to convey the information to interest an agent in requesting your book proposal.

Finally, please keep in mind that agents (and publishers) can be particular, so ask how an agent prefers submissions.

You typically only get "one shot" so you need to send your best, edited work. No agent or publisher will be inclined to take on a slip-shod, unedited submission. Many authors assume they can always "fix things up" later. This is not how the real publishing world works. You must submit a clean, edited proposal and manuscript in order for your work to be considered.

4.

Finding a Publisher

There are different types of publishers in the literary industry, including "publishers" who want to be paid by the author. I will start with these fee-based, vanity or self-publishing companies. There are also "subsidy" or "collaborative" publishers which will be discussed below — followed by traditional publishers.

Types of Publishers

Self-publishing involves publishing a book without the benefit of a traditional, "real" publisher. All of the production costs for the book are absorbed by the author. Self-publishing has been around for a long, long time, and has a place in the history of literature. Originally, people who owned printing presses published their own books (as well as essays, newspapers, etc.). As times changed, and publishing houses sprung into existence, self-publishing became less popular, though it has always been around. More recently, self-publishing has seen a surge in popularity with the advent of digital printing. This technology has made it easier and less expensive to print books. One of the most common forms of this newer technology is Print-on-Demand, often referred to by its acronym, P.O.D. Print-on-Demand saves money, because books are only printed when they are needed, as opposed to the "regular" offset printing utilized by most traditional publishers.

In self-publishing, an author has a contractual agreement with a company making most of their money through fees paid to them by the author. Because anyone can contract with this type of press, and therefore be published, most people in the literary industry don't consider self-published books to be "legitimate" books. This is due, in part, to the lack of selectivity (whereas, traditional publishers are extremely selective, and it is highly competitive to be published). In addition, the majority of distributors, wholesalers, and retailers won't carry books printed by self-publishing presses. The end result is that the author usually isn't able to sell their book in large enough quantities to even recoup the fees paid to the company, making self-publishing a financially poor route to go, usually.

The differences between self-publishing and vanity publishing are almost non-existent in today's world — and are looked upon in much the same way in the literary industry. In self-publishing, the author probably has more say-so than in vanity publishing. But the author also has to perform all of the functions to bring the book out on their own. In addition to writing the book, this includes such tasks as editing, layout, art work, jacket design, marketing, etc. The only aspects the author doesn't have to usually worry about are finding a printer, and having the books bound, but the author will still need to figure out where to store any inventory. The author also typically has to worry about copyrighting the book and securing an ISBN number.

Often times, after all of this headache, the quality of the books produced by self-publishing presses is not quite as good, either. This is another deterrent to the distributors, wholesalers, and retailers. Nobody is inclined to carry a substandard product, even if the pages contain beautiful prose.

Many people have an "attitude" about self or vanity publishing. It seems to imply that the writer isn't professional. And this stigma can be interpreted to mean that the author was incapable of getting an agent or publisher. Therefore, the implication is that the book must be no good.

In fact, a large number of individuals who toil in the literary world are reticent regarding self-publishing presses. While self-published and vanity press books are occasionally picked up by "real" publishers, it is rare. Probably one of the best-known self-published books is the erotic romance novel, *Fifty Shades of Grey*, by British author E.L. James which was eventually picked up by a "legitimate" publisher. However, this is still an infrequent occurrence. Generally, agents and traditional publishers don't give self-published authors the time of day.

There are also a growing number of "subsidy" or "collaborative" publishers. This type of publishing differs slightly from self-publishing in that the author shares the book production costs with the publishing house. There are even some large, traditional publishers that have subsidy imprints or divisions now.

The primary advantage of subsidy publishing over self or vanity publishing is that there is still an element of selectivity in the process. In other words, not every author can be published, despite their willingness to share in the costs. Hence, distributors, wholesalers, and retailers are more inclined to carry the book. Nonetheless, authors can still be in for hefty fees (though the fees are less than the self-publishing, fee-based models, especially in the cases where the collaborative publisher also uses lower cost printing technology).

With all of this said, there are more and more traditional publishers moving to Print-on-Demand technology, so you shouldn't necessarily be wary of publishers based on the kind of printing used. If a publisher doesn't charge fees, uses P.O.D., and seems able to keep up with order fulfillment in the retail market, there probably isn't any concern.

One method I use to determine if a smaller publisher is legitimate (as opposed to a vanity or self-publishing press) is to question them about their relationships and accounts with the various distributors and retailers. If they don't have the appropriate relationships, there is usually something wrong — and they are probably not a "real" publisher. In my opinion, it is generally a waste of time to write a book if nobody (other than close friends and family) will ever be able to read it. And the only books that have a chance to be read in any numbers are found in libraries or book stores (including online retailers).

However, there are times when it might make sense to self-publish. For instance, there are some people who have led extraordinary or interesting lives, but aren't famous (so it is unlikely that traditional publishers would take an interest in their life stories). These types of people might want to write an autobiography so that their friends, and family members through the generations will know about their special accomplishments and unusual tales.

Or, perhaps someone is an expert in a narrow area, or works in an extremely specialized field. Because there wouldn't be wide enough interest in such a book, agents and publishers would be reticent to take on such a niche project. However, it might be advantageous to "publish" a book in an obscure area so that colleagues who work in the same field can benefit from the author's knowledge.

Many self-publishers only publish e-books, and no matter how the book is published, it should be noted that e-books are here to stay, and as such, they should now be considered one of the options in publishing. In fact, as of this writing, e-books are a growing segment of the literary industry, whereas "physical" book sales are declining. There are quite a few legitimate publishers who are only producing e-books, and many authors are meeting with considerable success. In addition, significant numbers of traditional publishing houses are producing e-book versions of their hardcover and paperback books. Part of the current struggle with e-books involves the myriad of technology "platforms" for all of the different e-book reading devices. In other words, Kindle isn't compatible with Nook. Nor are they compatible with books sold in the Apple store, etc. At some point, I think the industry will need to work on making e-books readable on all of the platforms, or they will be forced to settle on one platform — but I'll save the rest of the predictions for someone with more technological know-how than me. Suffice it to say, e-books are not going away.

From an agent's vantage point, we have very little to do with the types of publishing discussed above (with the exception of e-books). Generally, we are concerned with helping authors get published by traditional publishers. Of course, there is some variation among traditional publishers too.

While all authors dreams of being published by the likes of Random House or Simon & Schuster (or any other large house), publishing companies come in all sizes with different advantages and disadvantages. I have had positive experiences with publishers that are big, small, and everything in between. I've also had a few unfortunate deals with not-so-good publishers along the way, but, often times, this was more a function of the specific people involved, rather than the particular publishing house.

There are good reasons to be published by the large

houses. They have a lot more money, and therefore, there is a higher probability of receiving an advance (more on advances later, though). Bigger publishers also have better resources and (sometimes) more reliable relationships with the retail market since they are better known. And, of course, any author's friends have heard of publishers such as HarperCollins or Penguin.

However, there are also benefits to being published by smaller houses, and I have represented many successful books put out by independent publishers over my career. Often times, these publishers are actually more willing to take a risk on first time authors or writers who lack any notoriety. They tend to be more "hands-on" — which sometimes leads to a better product. And, acquiring editors at smaller houses often have a more personal relationship with the author and agent. All of this is possible due to the fact that the independent publishers have less titles to worry about in any given period, and the companies usually have less bureaucratic layers. While most of these publishers don't give out advances (or the advances are relatively small), sometimes they are actually more generous with royalties than those found in the big houses.

Almost all the large publishers require that an author be represented by an agent, and a substantial number of independent publishers do, as well. In fact, a good number of publishers won't even talk to writers without their agents present, and many publishers only communicate through the agent.

Locating a Publisher

So, how do agents locate a publisher for an author? The answer is probably obvious, but I'll spell out the process anyway. I, of course, can only speak to the way in which my company works, but I'm sure it's similar to that of other agencies.

After we have agreed to rep a writer, and they have signed an agency agreement, we begin the process by making a long "hit list" of those publishers we believe might be interested in the particular work. I have extensive computer files on every publisher I have had any kind of contact with over the years. The files include information on their likes and dislikes, as well as the genres in which they work. I keep comments from acquiring editors about previous works they have reviewed — which can sometimes give me guidance regarding the viability of subsequent works I am representing. Sometimes I even have notes about certain personality traits of particular editors to be sure that I don't interact with them regarding manuscripts on topics they might find offensive, or contrary to their political views, etc.

The list of potential publishers includes big, medium, and small houses. We begin to narrow the list as we phone and email publishers (depending upon their preferences for how they like to be contacted). If the acquiring editor is interested enough to take a look at the book proposal and/or manuscript, the material is typically sent to them via email. There are a few exceptions where an editor will want a hard copy of the work, and these are usually sent by an overnight service such as UPS or FedEx. Occasionally, I also meet with publishers in-person to discuss a project, and this usually indicates an extremely high level of interest.

We try to contact as many publishers as possible in the same time frame. This is so that we can get a feel for whether there is any chance of enticing more than one publisher to make an offer. If there is broad enough enthusiasm, we conduct an "auction" among the interested parties — hoping to drive up the advance. This occurs infrequently, though. Most authors find that they only have interest from one publisher.

In fact, it can take a relatively long time to find the right fit with a publisher under normal circumstances. This is due (I think) to the enormous amount of reading acquiring editors have on their desks at all times, in addition to all of their other duties. As an agent, I can relate to the never-ending piles of time-consuming reading!

Once an agent has sent an editor a book proposal, it is usually considered inappropriate to "bug" them about it unless there is overwhelming, immediate interest by a number of publishers (which could lead to an auction). As a result, this excruciatingly slow process can give new meaning to the saying, "Patience is a virtue."

In addition to refraining from bothering editors who have agreed to review an author's work, it is typically not permissible to resubmit "improved" versions of an author's work to the same publishing house if the first version has already been turned down. Therefore, it is imperative that authors put their best foot forward from the beginning. In other words, you get one chance with a publisher, so the material submitted to the agent to "shop" to publishing houses should be your best work. Think of it like an exam in school. If you got a "C" on the test, the teacher didn't tell you that you could retake the exam in case you could get an "A" the second time around.

Unfortunately, while an author is waiting patiently for an offer from a publisher, the author will usually experience some rejection from uninterested editors. Most publishers send their "critiques" by email, and I simply forward the emails to the author so they can see exactly what the publisher's reasoning is for passing on the opportunity to publish. It can be important for authors to have thick skin throughout this process.

The good news is, given enough time, most authors I choose to represent eventually end up published. Nevertheless, there are those occasional manuscripts that never see the light of day. Even I end up scratching my head. The author shouldn't be too hard on themselves — or their agent. There are an unending number of reasons why some books don't sell. Sometimes books don't sell because there's a similar book about to be released, or the topic of the book isn't considered currently viable, or something has changed in the world since the manuscript was written, or almost any other reason on earth. If your agent isn't able to find a publisher for your first work, you always have the option of trying another manuscript, or trying another agent who might have different contacts. Despite the seemingly huge number of books printed every year, it is still a select group of writers who actually get book contracts with legitimate publishers. Keep writing. It eventually pays off.

5.

The Publishing Contract & the Financial Side

After an author receives a verbal offer from a publisher, a contract will be prepared by the publishing house. Your agent will negotiate the terms of the agreement on your behalf and review the contract with you. Verbal offers are quite general, and typically only cover the financial structure, approximate length of the book, and when the final version of the manuscript will need to be submitted to the publisher. Therefore, it is important to assess all the clauses in the contract carefully.

Most authors seem primarily concerned with the financial side of the publishing agreement, so we will begin with the money. Authors should understand that there is wide variance from publisher to publisher, and sometimes within a particular house, in the amount of money paid to writers. As a result, it can be difficult to coherently discuss financial matters in this industry. Therefore, in an effort to demonstrate how the financial structure usually works, I will use high-end figures for the sake of illustration. Please keep in mind that most authors will not necessarily receive as generous a pay-out as my example below.

Advances

The first consideration on the financial side of a publishing agreement is the advance — or whether the author will receive an advance. Most writers dream of huge, multi-million-dollar checks coming from publishers as soon as they have signed a contract. They have read about these advances in newspapers, heard about them on TV news, and they have even seen fictional characters in movies act as though retirement is around the corner after they get their fat check for their book. Friends and colleagues brag about their payments from publishers, and wanna-be authors drool at the mere thought.

Unfortunately, most of the above is fiction, or vastly exaggerated. The sad truth is that the majority of authors are advanced little or no money by the publishing house. Unless you are a celebrity, notorious for some reason, a KNOWN expert in your field, or simply get lucky, the chances of receiving a substantial advance are probably as likely as winning the lottery. Bear in mind that even without an advance, a publisher is still making an investment in an author. They have to pay their editors, jacket designers, marketing people, etc., and they have book production and printing costs. Publishers still take a financial risk each time they acquire a first-time or unknown writer's work.

However, sometimes the moon and stars are aligned, and a publisher feels generous. If there is an advance (of any size), authors should know that the word "advance" means exactly what it sounds like. In other words, the publisher is advancing money to the author, and that money has to be earned back based on the royalty structure before any actual royalties will be paid. In addition, most often, advances aren't paid in one lump sum. Traditionally, advances are paid in three installments, with each payment tied to a particular stage in the publishing process. The first part of the advance is normally due upon the execution of the publishing agreement (which could actually mean that the publisher has to deliver a check for the amount due within ninety days of executing the contract). The second benchmark for the next portion of the advance is usually the period referred to as "delivery and acceptance" of the manuscript. This means a check will be cut (within ninety days) when the author submits the manuscript ON TIME, and the publisher agrees the work reflects what the publisher was expecting. The final advance check is typically due (within ninety days) of the actual publication date of the book.

The date for the third advance payment can be a little tricky. This is due to the fact that books are rarely released on time. Sometimes the books are published earlier than predicted, but more often than not, book releases are delayed because of factors beyond the control of the author or the agent. Books go through many stages in order to be published, and inevitably, something or someone causes a delay. Authors are late turning in the manuscript; authors are late turning back in their edited page proofs; editors have a crisis with another author; printing presses break; books ship through the distribution system more slowly than anticipated; etc. So, the final advance is due whenever the book is finally published.

As mentioned earlier, advances must be earned back before any royalties can be collected. Consequently, I believe authors place too much emphasis on the importance of advances. If you think about it for a minute, unless the publisher is advancing the author more money than the book can earn (which is unlikely), the advance is a "wash" financially. If the advance is based on potential earnings, and the publisher has evaluated the book's potential reasonably well, the author may never collect any money beyond the advance.

Royalties

In fact, the reverse is also true. If an author's book does well enough, even without an advance, they will make good money — which brings me to royalties. Like advances, there is usually a three-tier system for royalties. And, again, royalties are tied to certain benchmarks. Please remember that what I am about to demonstrate is based upon generous royalties not found in significant numbers of contracts.

In my example, the publisher will pay ten percent of the retail list price of the book (usually based on the net profit to the publisher) for the first five thousand books sold. They then will pay twelve and a half percent of the list price (net to the publisher) for the next five thousand books sold. Finally, the author will be paid fifteen percent (net to publisher) for the life of the book after the first ten thousand books are sold. Please note that there are always exceptions to the standard royalty structure, such as books sold through book clubs, etc. However, this detailed discussion should be saved for a conversation between you and your agent when you are offered a publishing agreement.

Royalties (and any other monies owed the author outside of the advance) are, for the most part, paid twice a year. Some publishing houses only reconcile accounts and send checks once a year, while a few publishers actually pay quarterly. This aspect of the publishing agreement is not negotiable. The author is simply beholden to whatever system the publishing house utilizes. When checks are cut for a work, all the money flows through the agent's escrow account. The agent takes their percentage off the top and disburses the rest of the funds to the author — and any other parties to the agency agreement such as illustrators or ghostwriters.

Bonuses

In addition to advances and royalties, occasionally there is an opportunity to negotiate a "bonus" in the publishing contract. This is an area where agents can be creative. Most bonuses I have been able to write into an agreement have been tied to best seller lists such as those in *The New York Times, The Washington Post,* or even a book's ranking on Amazon. For instance, an author might earn an extra five thousand dollars if their book remains in any position on *The Post's* list for more than a certain number of weeks. There are lots of ways to structure these clauses, though they are pretty rare.

Fulfilling the Contract

Beyond the money, there are still a myriad of "issues" to be concerned about in publishing contracts. First and foremost, the author should be certain the delivery date for the manuscript is realistic, especially if the writing isn't finished when a publishing offer is made. Publishers REALLY frown upon receiving the manuscript late, and some have been known to cancel the agreement due to tardiness. Even litigation hasn't helped authors in this area. Of course, in a strictly contractual look at this issue, an author who doesn't meet the agreed upon delivery date in the agreement is clearly in breach. Therefore, don't agree to any deadlines which cannot be met.

The same can be said about the length of the work. Most contracts identify the length of the book by a word count since the number of pages can vary depending upon the dimensions of the physical book. Authors should NOT agree to an unrealistic word count in the publishing agreement. If you need a lot of words to get your message across, don't underestimate. In the other extreme, if you write succinctly, be sure you don't have to fill up pages with meaningless drivel.

However, authors do need to exercise some flexibility, or they may never be able to get published. So, if your manuscript in its current form is forty thousand words, but the publisher wants fifty thousand words, it is probably best to "find" another ten thousand words. In the same vein, if you think you need another seven months to complete your manuscript, but the publisher offering you a deal would like everything turned in by six months, it's a good idea to rearrange your schedule so you can meet the publisher's deadline. Without the author demonstrating some reasonableness, publishers will move on to the next author's book.

Publishing Date

Authors should also be aware of the timeframe in which the book will be published and hit the retail market. As discussed earlier, publishers aren't always able to bring a book out on schedule, but authors need to be prepared for their work's release. After their manuscript has been delivered, and the publisher's edits are incorporated, the author should begin thinking about how they will market and publicize the book. This means the author needs to be available. Therefore, if you have planned your next overseas vacation around the time the book will initially find its way into stores, it is not a good idea to sign an agreement implying you will be ready to promote the book.

Subsequent Works

There are so many other areas to be aware of in publishing agreements, but I will only cover some of those here to give you a feel for why every author should be careful (and sure of decent representation) before putting their signature on a contract. For example, most agreements have a clause addressing subsequent books by the same author. Some of these clauses can end up looking rather onerous if the first book doesn't go well, and the author has had a less than pleasing experience with the publisher. Therefore, it's important to make sure there is some sort of "out" for the author for future books, even if the ability to eventually get to another publisher is cumbersome. Often times, the best an author can do is to work out language that allows their original publisher a right of first refusal. And if no agreement can be reached after negotiating in "good faith" for a period of time, the author has the right to look for a different publisher. If an offer is made, the author usually has to go back to their initial publisher — who has the right to match the offer. There are, of course, some "creative" ways to make these "tie you up for life" clauses better sometimes, but it depends upon who the publisher is, and who you have as your representative.

Indemnity

Indemnity clauses can also be a major concern in certain kinds of books. The more there is a possibility of being sued (e.g., if you are writing a "kiss and tell", etc.), the more important these clauses become. Publishers will only "give" so much in most cases, but again, good representation is a must.

Rights

Various "rights" issues can be extremely important depending upon the author, the book, and the particular publisher. These rights run a range from foreign to film and television to stage plays, etc. If your book is not conducive to any of these areas, you probably have less of a concern, but most books have at least a possibility in one of these areas. The question to be decided is whether the author should try to retain the rights in any of these areas, or whether it makes sense to leave the rights with the publisher (and share the money if the book is made into a movie, etc.). There are times when it is best to allow the publisher to remain in charge of these areas since they may have more experience or contacts. This is something that should be discussed between the author and their agent.

Other types of issues include clauses addressing how much material in the book can be used by the author for other purposes. For instance, if your book's topic relates to your professional work, you want to be certain you are able to utilize enough material from your book for professional conferences, published industry papers, etc. without violating the publishing agreement.

Author Copies

And, I know firsthand that every author is worried about how many free books they will receive from their publisher. While I would encourage authors to make their friends, family, and colleagues purchase their book since these people are the author's easiest market, every author will need books to send to possible media or organizations hosting book signings. There is a lot of discrepancy from publisher to publisher. I know one publisher that agrees to twenty books for the author, but many publishers are far more stingy — agreeing to as few as three free books. And some even none at all.

In the end, nobody can be certain of what will be found in any given publishing agreement. However, it is vitally important for authors to have good, professional representation. If your agent doesn't have a law degree, it usually makes sense to have an attorney review the publishing agreement. However, your attorney should be someone who has knowledge about the standards, norms, and customs in the literary world — rather than the man or woman who handled your divorce or took on your automobile accident case. Just as other industries have their peculiarities, so does the book world, and you should only be represented by someone familiar with this area.

Finally, like so many things in life, it is often necessary to “pick your battles” in negotiating a publishing contract. Prioritize those items that are most important, because it is unlikely you will be afforded every change requested. After all, publishers are in the driver’s seat, and you don’t want to be run off the road — left with no possibility of even being published.

6.

Book Promotion

Writing a book, finding an agent, and getting published are just the beginning of your literary journey. The real work starts when authors have to promote their work, and it isn't as easy as it may seem. Every author I speak with, almost without exception, tells me about all of their ideas and contacts for selling their book should it be published. Unfortunately, most of these grandiose ideas never actually come to fruition. I don't think this is necessarily due to any faults inherent with authors. I do believe it is simply difficult — with many obstacles to overcome.

Publicity

An author's first problem is usually related to an unrealistic impression that the publisher will be busy scheduling appearances for them on big, national media shows. This rarely happens, so get this thought out of your head now. Publishers do have contacts in the media, but they also have a lot of authors and titles. Publicity departments are overwhelmed in publishing houses — with too many books to publicize at any given time.

In addition, and related to the volume of titles requiring publicity, there are only so many times publishing publicists can go back to the same trough. In other words, if a publicist for Simon & Schuster gets an author on *Good Morning America*, it will probably be a while before GMA will agree to have another Simon & Schuster writer on their program. After all, the media has a myriad of ways to find guests for their programming, and they are unlikely to put all their eggs in one basket.

Furthering the difficulty for authors is the fact that most media is highly focused on "breaking news" — which means that it can be difficult for writers to be invited on shows in the first place. Unless your book has a "hook" related to breaking news, or you are a recognized expert in the subject matter of the breaking news, it can be near-impossible to get on national programs.

Now that you understand it would be unwise to rely only upon a publicist employed by a publishing house, let's focus on some realistic strategies for promoting a book.

Book Tours

In general, book tours, like so many other aspects of the literary industry, are not always accurately portrayed in films and television shows. Most authors will not meet with success if they embark upon a two- to three-week marketing and publicity campaign. This just isn't a long enough period of time to get the word out — and create a buzz. Instead, promoting a book is a process, and well-selling authors participate in the process for lengthy amounts of time — even as long as a year. Obviously, this doesn't mean an author needs to quit their job, and roam the country attempting to market their book. Rather, authors should continuously look for promotion opportunities, and seize those chances when they are presented. It is always beneficial to have a big "push" when the book is initially published, but it is equally important to continue to publicize the book as it becomes more dated in order to keep sales (and royalties) flowing.

There are three primary areas on which authors should focus their publicity efforts: traditional media (including local and national), in-person book signings before live-audiences (who will purchase books), and all things Internet-related. All three aspects are important, and none should be excluded from your campaign.

Believe it or not, traditional media probably has the most impact on book sales. This is due to the fact that you get the most bang for your buck. Even a poorly rated TV or radio audience has more viewers or listeners than the average size of any other kind of audience. While it is unrealistic to think that everyone who tunes in will buy a book, experience shows a good boost in sales after an author appearance. Securing media "hits" can be difficult, especially if you are a non-celebrity, first-time author. Therefore, authors should consider hiring a publicist familiar with the media and promoting books. Good publicists can be hard to come by — many of them take your money and produce no results. So, ask questions, and compare pricing. Often times, your agent or publisher can make a recommendation — or many agencies have a division which does publicity.

Book Signings

Book signing events also can be difficult to line up. Much of society is only interested in attending events with celebrities, and if you aren't a household name or notorious, you will be faced with a good deal of rejection. I have even seen some celebrities struggle in this area. However, all of this means that unknown authors simply have to work harder at tracking down events — and must have extremely thick skin to deal with the turn-downs. Don't let it bother you when book stores, companies, or other organizations won't host a signing. Be determined and find a nexus between your book and an organization's mission so that they will be thrilled to have you appear.

This is an area where everyone has possible contacts. Friends, family, employers, and colleagues can all be helpful. Everyone knows other people. Tap into these resources and ask people you know to host book signing events. If you belong to a club or organization, or if you participate in non-profit or charity work, find out if you can have a book event. I think most authors are surprised by the kindness (and helpfulness) of those people they already know. People are proud of friends who successfully get a book published, and these same people often want to be a part of the process.

Online Promotion

The Internet affords quite a few opportunities for authors. At the very least, all authors should have a website devoted to their book. If you have a website about something other than your book, the two sites should be linked, but you shouldn't just put your book on your existing site. In addition, all of the social networking sites, such as Facebook, Twitter, and Instagram can be handy tools for promoting books. The Internet is exploding with programming, too. While there are some major players on the Internet now, there are more and more smaller media shows to explore — and many of these are willing to interview first-time authors. Creating a blog can sometimes be productive, but if you decide to blog, please remember to post with enough frequency so that there is a chance of creating a following. In addition to writing your own blog, organized blog campaigns can have an impact. In this case, the author enlists friends and family to go on existing blog sites (with themes that relate to the book), and the "helpers" work the book into the blog conversation. Finally, it can be beneficial to link your book website to any other sites on the Internet. Talk to your friends, family, and colleagues. Some of them will happily put a link to your website.

In summary, try to capitalize on all three areas available for promotion. Call in favors from friends, family, and colleagues. Consider all opportunities that come your way. Don't give up just because some attempts at publicity don't pan out. If possible, hire a publicist to assist you, and ask your agent for advice. While agents are NOT publicists, they have a lot of experience, and are usually well connected.

You can enhance your chances for successful promotion of your book if you keep this aspect of the literary process in mind while you are writing your book. Think about possible news hooks and elaborate on these hooks in the book. Not all of your ideas will resonate with the media, but some of them might catch the eye of a producer, booker, or even a host.

In the end, be creative, and try new ways to promote your book. Work the phones, send emails, and even become a "pest" to get the help you deserve. Any way you can reach a new book buyer helps the overall picture. It can take time to build a platform to get noticed. Keep at it. I bet you will be glad when you get that first break.

7.

Industry Issues

The talented American poet, Maya Angelou, once said, "All great achievements require time." Nothing could be truer in the literary world. Getting a book published doesn't happen overnight, and at times, it can seem as though the process moves at a snail's pace — if it moves at all. Unfortunately, this tortoise-like rapidity often results in delays across the publishing process — which can have a direct impact on authors. In addition, sometimes a delay in one area can result in lengthy delays in other areas. In order for a book to be released in the retail market, there are a lot of different people who need to be involved, and the aftermath can leave an author feeling frustrated and helpless. Publishing is constantly wrought with troublesome issues. I thought it would be beneficial to discuss some of the problems, so you are aware of the pitfalls.

As you may have gathered by the statements above, publishers are not great at hitting the targeted release date for a book. Occasionally, the trouble actually begins with the author. Writers are notorious for missing contractual deadlines to submit their manuscripts. When this occurs, if the publisher agrees to ignore the breach of the publishing agreement and proceed with the book, every aspect of the process is delayed.

Of course, there are also a plethora of areas that can cause delays on the publishing side of the fence. Editors can get behind in their work, and that pushes the whole process back. The length of the delay might relate to the amount of editing needed for a particular work — or other manuscripts requiring major edits can result in your book being put on the back burner.

Printer delays appear to be relatively common, too. Unfortunately, much of this is outsourced by publishing houses, so there's not much that can be done to facilitate a quicker print run. Like all machinery and technology, printing equipment breaks down, and the only option for everyone involved is to wait for the press to be fixed.

Because many retailers get their inventory of books through distributors, glitches in the distribution process can also cause books to be delayed in reaching stores. Books are heavy. Therefore, cartons of books heading to the retailers usually ship by ground — which can take a while. And, once the books reach their destination, the store has to account for the number of books, and physically shelve them in the case of "brick and mortar" locations.

Much to the dismay of authors, agents aren't typically able to do much to help in any of these scenarios. Agents don't have accounts with the distributors, and clearly, agents aren't employed by the retailers. Ultimately, the only assistance an agent can lend is to "bug" the publisher to be proactive to hunt down where and why a delay has occurred — and to encourage the publisher to push others to move as quickly as possible.

Because of the nature of the publishing industry, it is not a good idea for an author to schedule book signing events, launch parties, or media interviews until everyone is sure the books have reached the retail market. After all, there really isn't any point to these promotion activities if there aren't books available for sale. However, as Thomas Jefferson once remarked, "Delay is preferable to error."

Even after books are for sale by retailers, this does not mean every author's book will be in every book store — nor does it mean every book will be sold by every on-line retailer on the Internet. Ultimately, it is up to the individual retailer to decide whether they wish to carry a specific title. Unless you are a celebrity, it can be difficult for publishers to convince all the store buyers to carry your book. In addition, even if a store agrees to stock your book, this doesn't necessarily mean the store will continue to carry the book. In fact, if copies of your book aren't selling well, the store will eventually return the books, and cease carrying the title. Amazon seems to be the only place where almost all titles are enthusiastically embraced.

Another concern for authors relates to getting proper support from book stores for book signing events. Many stores simply won't do "off-site" events. Therefore, authors should talk to stores well in advance of any events to insure there will be a store present to sell the books during an appearance. Authors usually have a lot of action in the geographic area where they reside, so it can be beneficial to form a long-term relationship with a book store in your hometown area. This can be productive for the author and the store — book stores often embrace the idea of working as the exclusive seller for an author in their area. Most book stores need three-to-four weeks' notice to insure they will have an adequate number of copies of the book for an author event (since stores don't stock large quantities, and therefore, the store must place an order before the event).

Again, while your agent can advocate for you, there's not much that can be done if book stores are contacted too late. And, agents do not control the distribution and shipping of books. So, plan ahead to allow enough time for books to get to where they need to be, and don't schedule anything until you know the books are in the retail system.

These "issues" are just a drop in the bucket in terms of all the areas that can go wrong in the literary industry. If you want to write and be published, you will need to learn to roll with the punches. I have encountered a lot of angry authors over the course of my career, and I do not think swearing at or threatening your agent or publisher enhances the experience — or produces results. Instead, use your agent to help resolve these issues, but don't beat up on anyone. People in the literary world are only human, and nobody is going to intentionally "ruin" your book, event, or interview. We all have the same goals in mind — SELL, SELL, SELL!

Finally, Abraham Lincoln put it best when he said, "Always bear in mind that your own resolution to succeed is more important than any other."

Speaking Engagements

The author, Diane Nine, is available for seminars, panels, and presentations. For contact information, please visit www.ninespeakers.com.

CPSIA information can be obtained
at www.ICGtesting.com
Printed in the USA
LVHW050716100121
675964LV00008B/986